MR THINKALOT'S FANTASTIC ... CE ... EY

WRITTEN AND ILLUSTRATED
BY I.M. MAYES

Published by Purple Parrot Publishing

Printed in the United Kingdom

First Printing, 2020

ISBN: Print: 978-1-912677-98-6

Purple Parrot Publishing

www.purpleparrotpublishing.co.uk

Edited by Viv Ainslie

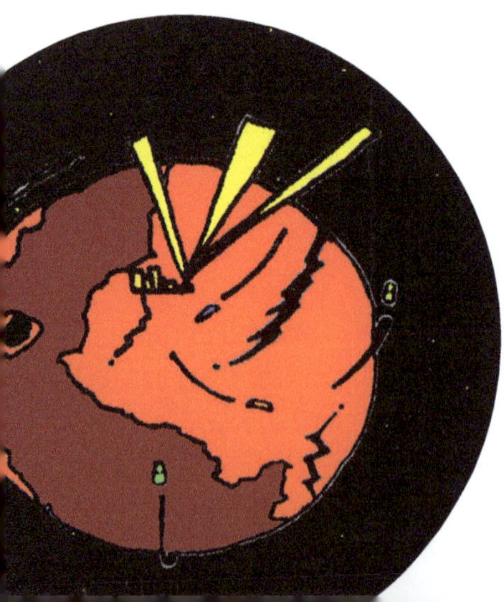

CONTENTS

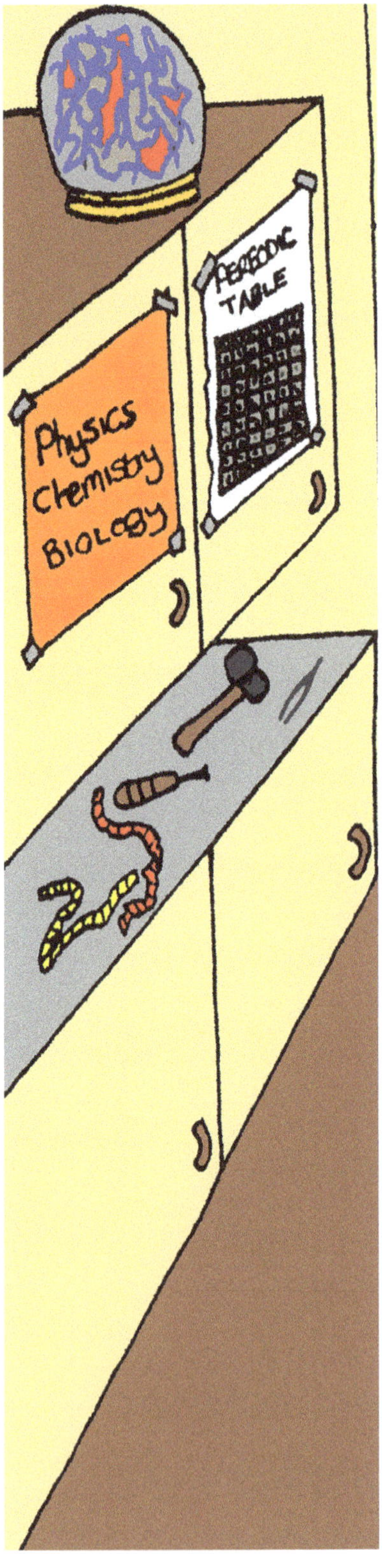
PERIODIC TABLE
Physics
Chemistry
BIOLOGY

CHAPTER 1

It's the year 2023. Mr Thinkalot is a science professor who lives in London. Mr Thinkalot has many fantastic inventions, theories and ideas but sadly, no one ever takes him seriously. He once suggested that there could be another solar system, identical to ours, far away from here; maybe even in another dimension. But no one listened; instead they laughed in his face and made fun of him.

Mr Thinkalot is fed up with people mocking him and has decided to stop listening to them altogether. What people don't know, is that he has been working on a *FANTASTICAL* new piece of equipment. He's been working on it secretly for years and is very close to finishing it but he's missing something - a vital piece of the puzzle.

Mr Thinkalot works for weeks without any sleep, using his periodic table, lots of different elements, chemicals and bits of technology to complete his *FABULOUS* new gadget. He puzzles over the problem for ages, brushing his ginger beard with his fingers.

Then it happens. *EUREKA* - a light bulb moment.

"Ahhh" Mr Thinkalot says, "that's what it needs!"

With his pliers, he adds an extra wire and a few more screws to his *BRILLIANT* invention. Then, letting out an excited laugh, he dances around the room "I've done it; I've finished it."

Suddenly, his eyelids begin to droop with tiredness. Realising he hasn't slept for weeks and just how tired he is, he throws a blanket over his *AMAZING* invention to cover it and makes his way to bed, banging into walls and tables along the corridor.

Crawling into his bed, he is very quickly asleep.

CHAPTER 2

He wakes the next morning with a spring in his step, excited to test his creation. He rushes downstairs, goes into the living room, and presses a secret button hidden under the candlestick on his fireplace.

The fireplace rotates 360 degrees, opening up into a small corridor. At the end of the corridor is a door. He walks down the corridor to the door, opens it and walks into his secret laboratory (it's his garage really but don't tell anyone).

Full of excitement, Mr Thinkalot pulls off the blanket covering his invention. He picks it up and says triumphantly "I will call you the **SUPER SPACE HELMET**."

"Right," he says, "it's time to see if my theories are correct and test this bad boy out."

Mr Thinkalot strides to the centre of the lab and places the SUPER SPACE HELMET over his head. With a big deep breath, he presses the POWER button. The helmet makes a low humming sound.

Then he presses BUTTON 1 and shouts, "activating camera mode; check."

Next, he presses BUTTON 2, "air supply; check."

Taking another deep breath, Mr Thinkalot gingerly presses BUTTON 3 "activating rocket boosters."

Suddenly, a draining sound, like a DOOOOOM noise, comes from the device as it powers down.

"Oh no! The power supply must have drained, it's completely out of juice," he sighs. "That means I need to go shopping."

Mr Thinkalot looks out of the window. It's pouring down with rain. "Great, just my luck," he mutters but he wastes no time. He rushes to the coat stand, picks up his lab coat and hat, throws them on and then jumps on his bike. Flicking the switch on his bicycle bell, he activates the hidden garage door. As it opens, he's away, peddling as fast as his legs can go. "I must get to the local store," he shouts while zooming along the road at top speed, ignoring all the bumps and potholes.

Finally, he arrives at the store, gets off his bike and opens the shop door. A couple of customers are pointing at him and laughing. He walks straight up to the counter.

"May I help you?" the shop keeper asks.

Mr Thinkalot hurriedly shouts, "yes, yes, I need all the batteries you have please?"

The shopkeeper looks at the other customers with raised eyebrows and then to Mr Thinkalot, "so why do you need all these batteries?"

Mr Thinkalot replies, "I am on the verge of something truly amazing! My top-secret science project."

The shop keeper and the other customers let out big belly laughs. "What have you ever achieved?" the shop keeper chuckles.

Mr Thinkalot doesn't answer. Dropping the money on the counter and swiping the batteries he whispers, "you'll see, you'll all see." He leaves the shop to the sound of more laughter.

Outside, the rain is still bouncing off the ground. Mr Thinkalot stuffs the batteries into his lab coat pockets, hops back on his bike and sets off for home. He peddles faster and faster; faster than on his journey to the shop, racing down the streets, eager to get back home.

As he arrives home, he flicks the switch on his bell to get back into his laboratory. He takes out the batteries from his coat pockets and puts them on his worktop. Putting his rain-soaked hat and lab coat onto the coat stand to dry out, he opens a cupboard and quickly reaches for a clean, dry lab coat and puts it on. Rushing to his **SUPER SPACE HELMET**, he clicks open the battery compartment, inserts 20 batteries and locks the cover into place. "Please, please don't fail me. I don't want to be a failure," he says as he ponders about the people who laughed at him at the shop.

Placing the **SUPER SPACE HELMET** gently over his head, he stretches his arms and legs, before attaching all the straps around his body and locking

them into place. Nervously, he takes a huge gulp of air and presses the **POWER** button on.

He presses **BUTTON 1** "activating camera mode; check."

Then he again presses **BUTTON 2** "activating air supply, check."

Sweat begins to run down his face as he swallows.

Taking in one last deep breath, he presses **BUTTON 3** "activating rocket boosters, all systems go," he announces.

An exciting sound comes from the **SUPER SPACE HELMET**. It goes **ZOOM WOW WOW, ZOOM WOW WOW** and in the blink of an eye and with a flash of light,

he is lifted off the ground. The lift off is so powerful that Mr Thinkalot rockets through the laboratory window at hypersonic speed.

Within a few seconds, his hometown shrinks right before his very eyes, as he rockets past some slightly scared birds and overtakes some planes. In no time at all, Mr Thinkalot is in the darkness of space. It's as if he had just jumped straight off the planet.

"I can hardly believe it; it works. Activate breaks."

Coming to a complete stop, floating above the

Earth, he exclaims, "Wow, it's so beautiful and breath taking," shedding a tear at the very sight.

It is completely mesmerising seeing our beautiful blue planet set amongst the blackest of space, with the glistening, glittering stars in the background; a truly amazing sight. Mr Thinkalot pinches himself on his arm just to make sure he's not dreaming.

CHAPTER 3

"Right, time to get on with my plans," Mr Thinkalot says to himself. "Activate light beams."

Two rays of light shine out of the helmet. He activates the rocket boosters again and shoots off higher and higher above the Earth. He passes the International Space Station and gives a little wave to the surprised astronauts staring at him from a porthole.

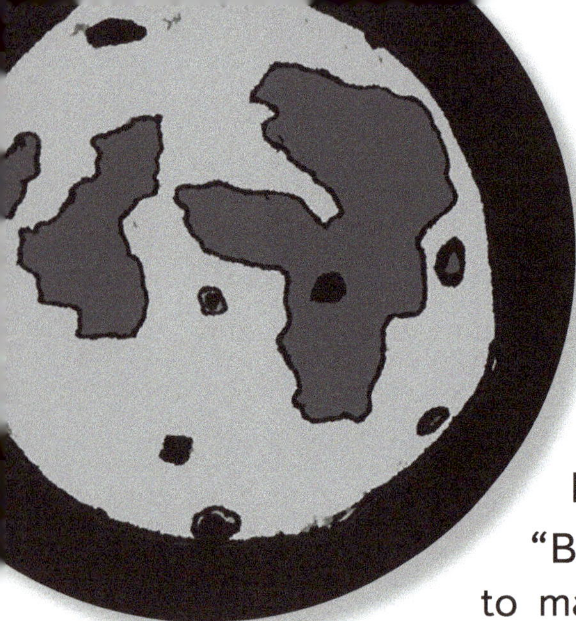

His little rockets take him past the moon. He can see all the craters and spots the Sea of Tranquility; if he wasn't travelling so fast, he might see the American Flag.

"Bert; set my trajectory to make a rotation of the sun and then on past all the planets in our solar system." Bert is the SUPER SPACE HELMET'S onboard computer!

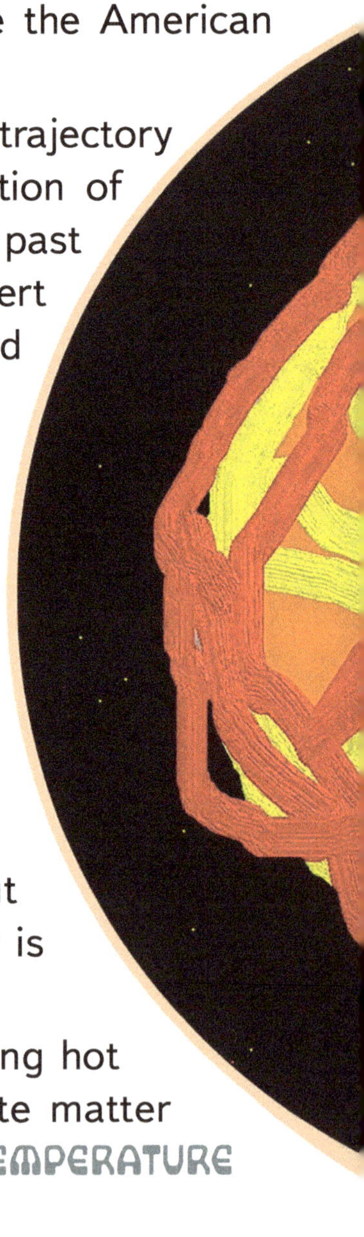

Bert announces, "JOURNEY SET," and blasts Mr Thinkalot off towards the sun.

As Mr Thinkalot always wants to know more about everything, he decides he wants to take a closer look at the huge star. He asks Bert to adjust his trajectory so he can get a bit nearer, which Bert does, but Mr Thinkalot finds that a bit nearer is actually a bit too close.

It starts getting really hot, like boiling hot and Bert confirms it by saying quite matter of factly, "WARNING, WARNING, TEMPERATURE CRITICAL."

Suddenly, aware that he is dangerously close to the sun, Mr Thinkalot makes a sharp turn back from danger and carries on with the 360-degree rotation around the sun. “So much heat, so much energy,” mumbles Mr Thinkalot.

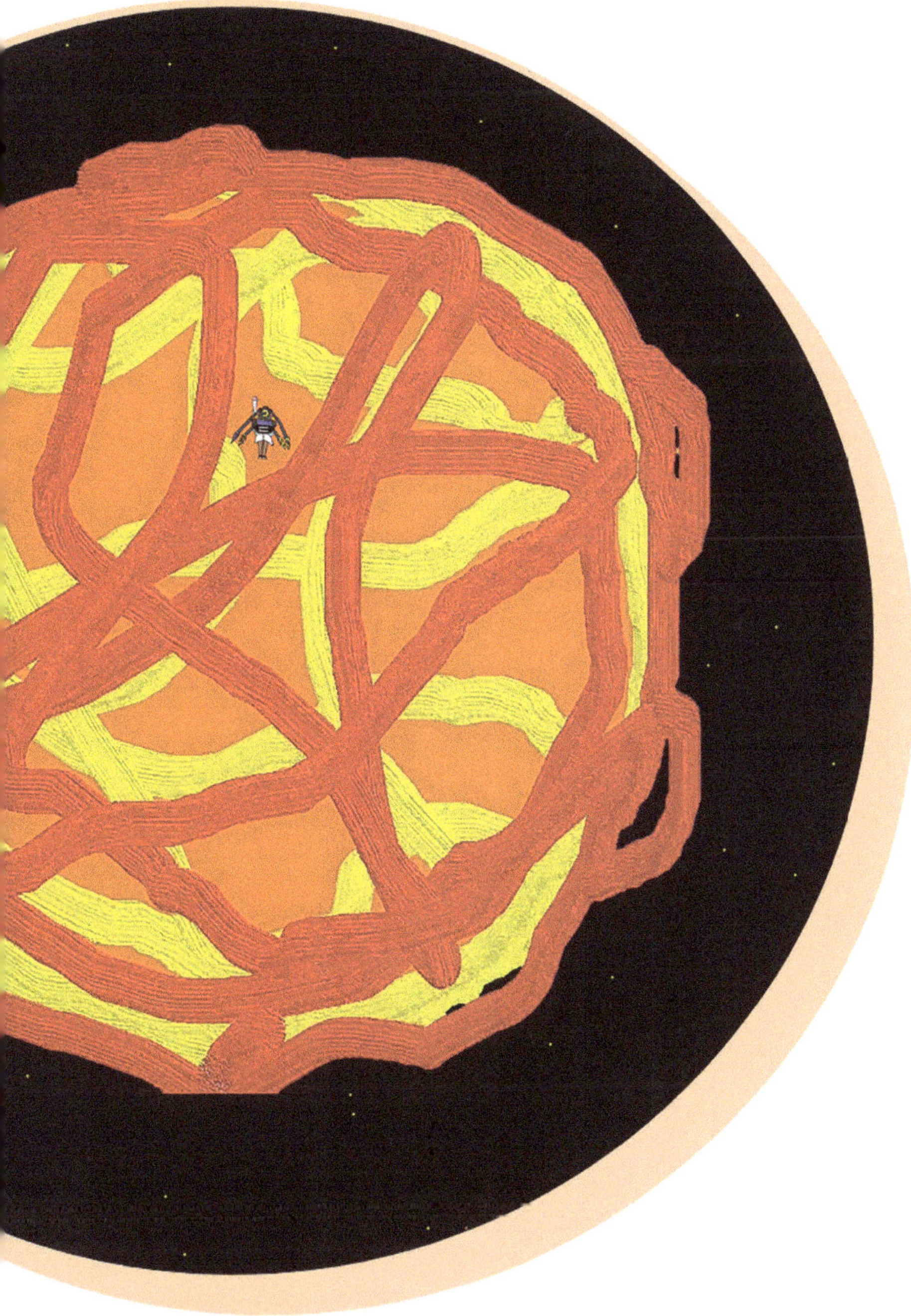

Once he is happy that he has seen all he needs of the sun, he carries on towards Mercury, the closest planet to the sun. It's not very interesting really, it looks a bit like the moon with lots of craters. As he passes it by on the darker side, away from the heat of the sun, he thinks that it's really very cold too. It's not long before he blasts past the second planet from the sun; Venus.

Mr Thinkalot says out loud, "Venus, you are very different up close! For the planet closest to our Earth, you are so very hot. Maybe that's why you are the brightest one we can see."

Leaving Venus behind, he sees Earth again and whispers, "Ah! The third planet from the sun; our beautiful Earth! You **ARE** the bluest of marbles in the vast, dark blackness of space."

Earth becomes so small so quickly as he races to the planet Mars. Mr Thinkalot is surprised and says, "it really is red too; well that's nice."

All of a sudden, Bert speaks in his monotone fashion, "WARNING, WARNING; ASTEROID BELT DETECTED."

In a panic, Mr Thinkalot shouts, "well avoid the asteroids Bert; avoid them."

The *SUPER SPACE HELMET* cleverly zigzags in and out of the gaps between the rocky asteroids perfectly. Mr Thinkalot cannot contain his excitement as he gains speed and blasts past Jupiter, Saturn, Uranus, Neptune and finally Pluto.

Amazed he has made it so far, he can't stop thinking of all the fantastic things he has seen: the planets, stars, satellites and the International Space Station.

He could never have imagined all of the vivid colours, the blackness and the sheer size of everything. All of it just open for discovery. His head is in a spin with thoughts whizzing around; lots of questions, ideas and theories.

Mr Thinkalot gets a little bit cross with himself and shouts "stop the thoughts; I must get on with my plan."

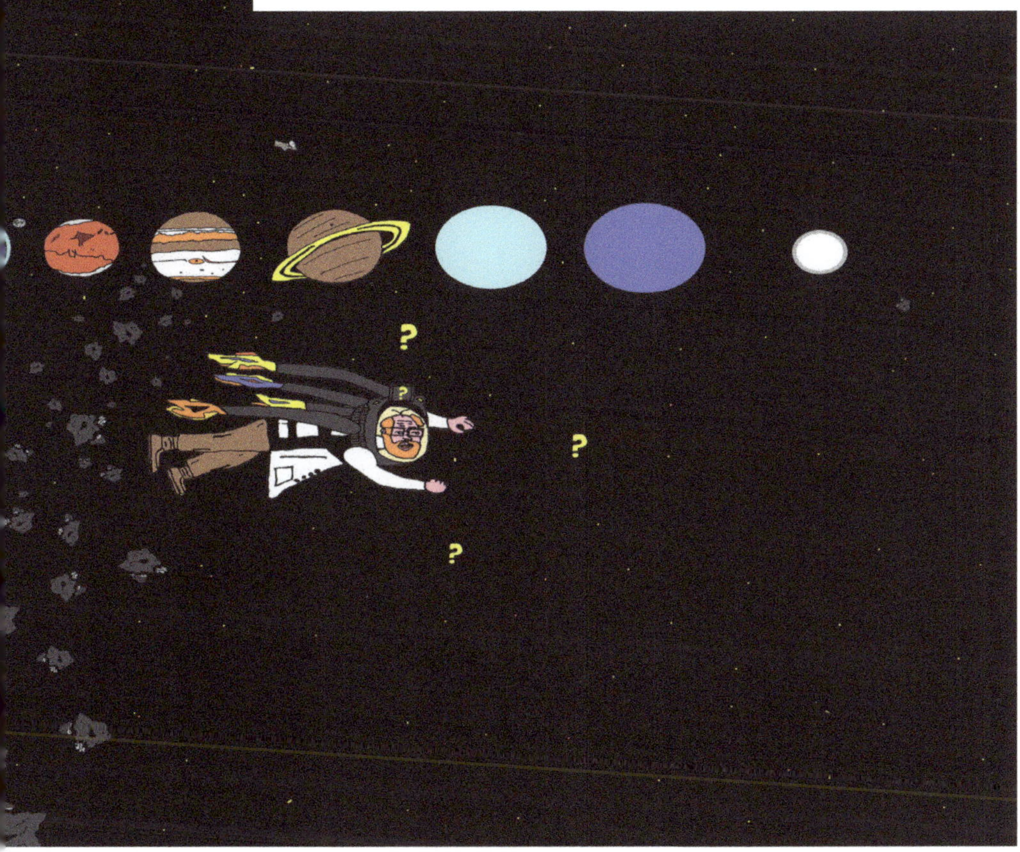

As he has been recording his whole journey with his onboard camera, he decides to leave a message for Earth.

"This is Mr Thinkalot, I am in deepest space and I have a message for everyone on Earth. I have reached further than any human ever has. I've seen beautiful things and wonders on my journey that you could only dream of. I designed my Super Space Helmet because I am impatient and need answers. My head races with questions and problems that I need answers to, so here I am.

I, Mr Thinkalot plan to enter a worm hole. I know this is dangerous but I'm inquisitive and as a professor of science I want to test my theories.

End of message."

Mr Thinkalot double blinks his eyes and Bert confirms, "DESTINATION MODE ACTIVATED."

A map opens up on his screen, clearly showing his location and all the planets he has passed in our solar system. Then he spots the worm hole and double blinks to select it.

"DESTINATION WORM HOLE SELECTED" Bert says in his very boring voice.

With the rocket boosters still going at full force, Mr Thinkalot heads towards the worm hole. He sees it in the distance rapidly getting closer and closer.

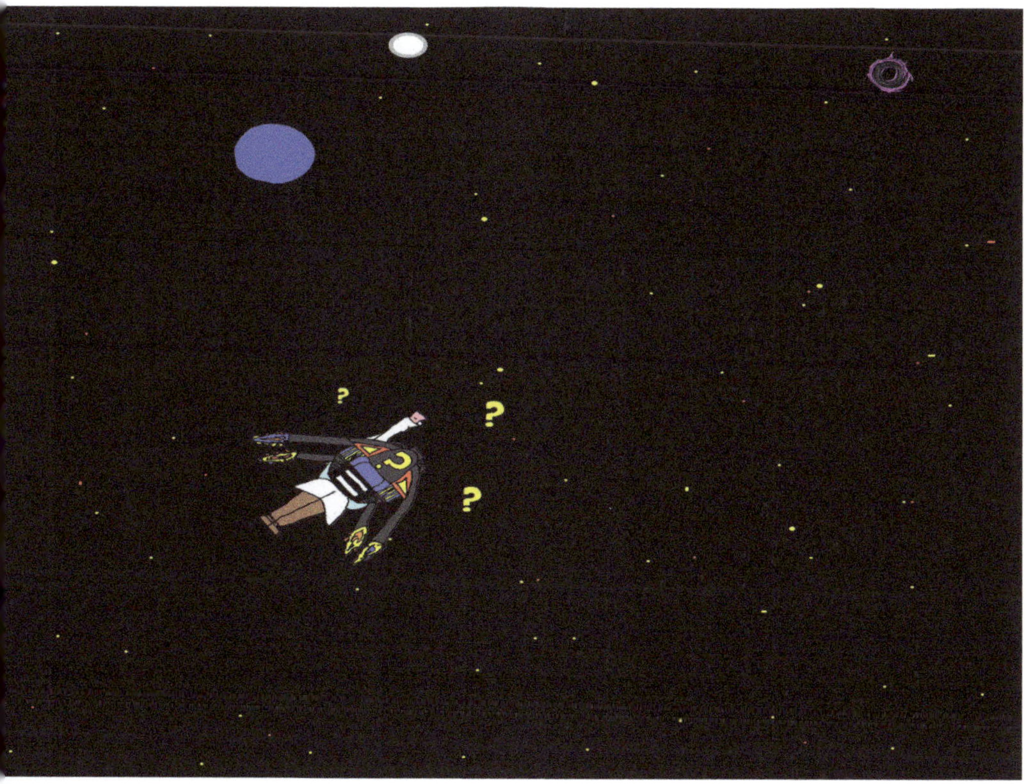

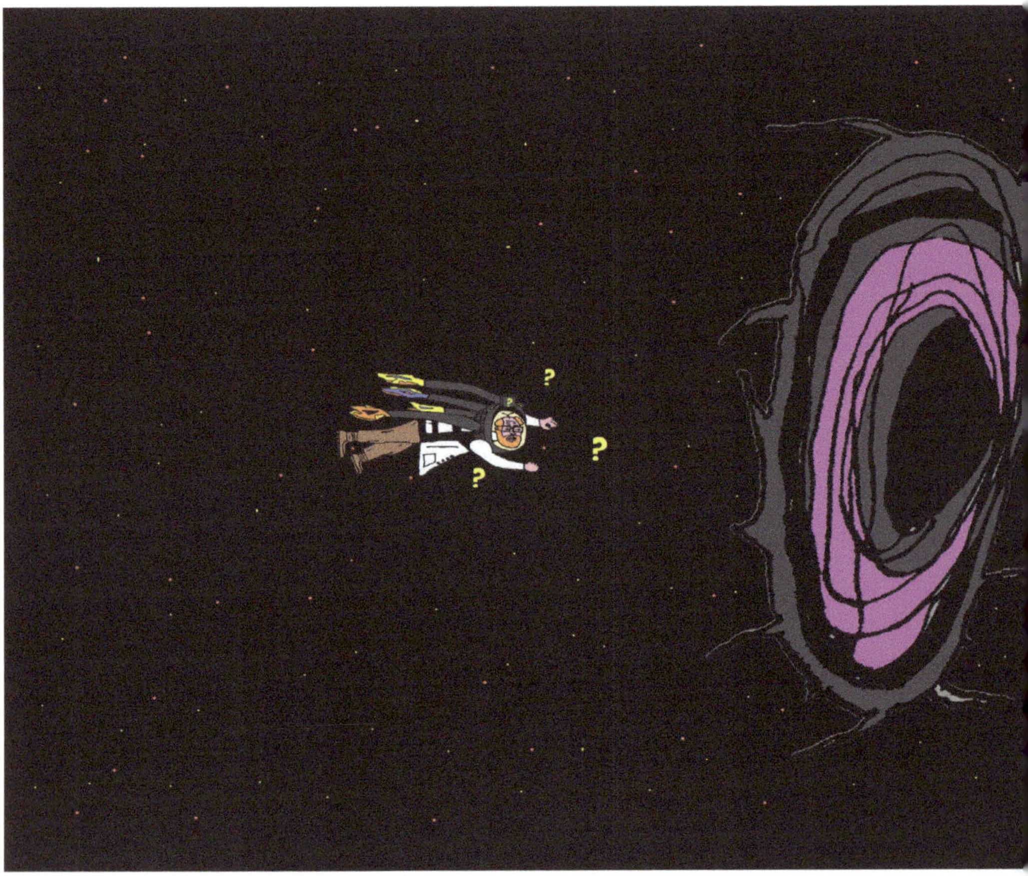

CHAPTER 4

As Mr Thinkalot gets closer to the worm hole, his fear and adrenaline kick in.

"The worm hole is so close now and it looks really scary; like a big open mouth ready to swallow me up," he comments.

SUDDENLY, the worm hole is right there in front of Mr Thinkalot.

Bert begins a countdown, "10,9,8,7,6,5,4,3,2,1." Usually, a countdown would be ***EXCITING*** but this is Bert, so it doesn't sound as exciting as it actually is.

Mr Thinkalot closes his eyes as the worm hole swallows him, then opens them the second he's in.

"I'm in a worm hole" he shouts.

He's floating and spinning around, faster and faster as if he's in a washing machine on the spin program, or like bath water being sucked down the plug hole.

Beautiful colours emerge from inside; every colour you could imagine from yellow to blue to red to green. Sparks, lights and flashes engulf him and blind him for a moment or two.

He lets out a scream, as he is suddenly spat out from the other end of the worm hole.

Mr Thinkalot is spinning out of control. In a panic he calls out "Bert, help: activate stabilisers."

The SUPER SPACE HELMET engages its stabilisers and brings him to a stop, much to his delight.

"Am I still alive Bert?"

"CONFIRMED," Bert replies.

Mr Thinkalot gazes around him to see what is out there. He cannot see a thing, just sheer black space.

"There's nothing to be seen here," he says "just empty space. We may as well go home".

An uninterested and very bored Bert suddenly announces, "UNIDENTIFIED PLANET LOCATED."

A ping activates on his screen showing him the location. Mr Thinkalot spins his head to look in that general direction and "Boom, there it is, I can see it," he yells, absolutely over the moon.

"Bert, lock onto that planet please."

It's nice that Mr Thinkalot is pleasant and polite to Bert but to be honest, Bert really doesn't care.

"LOCKED ON," Bert responds.

Mr Thinkalot aims himself towards the new planet as his boosters activate and push him on. As he nears the planet, he decides to record another message to log the information.

"To everyone on Earth.

This is so exciting. I have arrived safely out of the other side of the worm hole and I, Mr Thinkalot, have discovered a new planet. It's a reddish colour, similar to Mars in appearance.

I will send more detail when I get it.

End message."

Mr Thinkalot, getting much closer to the new planet, goes quiet for a few moments; he is completely blown away.

"I think I see what looks like a city, a golden city all lit up brightly. Wait, wait... Oh my, was that a flying vehicle?" he exclaims as he spots movement in the sky above the planet. "Have I discovered other life?"

Double blinking his eyes, he targets an area on the planet to land discreetly, about a mile away from the golden city.

Bert responds, "DESTINATION CONFIRMED."

The rocket boosters activate, hurtling him towards the planet. He enters the planet's airspace, then shouts "disengage rocket boosters." Bert complies sending Mr Thinkalot into a freefall down towards the planet.

"Activate parachute please Bert," he begs.

"PARACHUTE ACTIVATED," affirms Bert.

A sleek parachute comes out from the back of the SUPER SPACE HELMET, opens up and nicely allows Mr Thinkalot to drift slowly down to land safely on the ground below.

"Store parachute," he requests and the parachute is hoovered up back into the SUPER SPACE HELMET and stored efficiently.

"I can't believe it; I'm standing on an undiscovered planet. Bert, we need to run some diagnostic tests, are all systems active?"

"SYSTEMS ARE ALL FULLY FUNCTIONING," Bert confirms.

Mr Thinkalot takes a gentle jump but rather than landing hard on the ground, he bounces and floats all over the place.

"Mmm. Not much gravity here. Bert, please analyse planet composition" he asks.

"ANALYSING PLANET; BEEP, BEEP, BOP. PLANET IS MAINLY MADE UP OF ROCK, NO OTHER LIFE FORMS FOUND IN THIS VICINITY. SMALL AMOUNTS OF OXYGEN ARE PRESENT IN THE ATMOSPHERE," announces Bert.

"Are you sure? There is a city, so it doesn't make sense," Mr Thinkalot replies.

"CONFIRMED, NOT ENOUGH OXYGEN FOR YOU TO BREATH MR THINKALOT."

This means that Mr Thinkalot must keep his *SUPER SPACE HELMET* on so he can breathe.

Mr Thinkalot searches the dark reddish landscape of the planet.

It's an apocalyptic scene; everything is made up of red sand and dust. He looks around for the golden city that he had spotted from space. Then suddenly, like a mirage in a desert, he spots the magnificent looking city. It is certainly something you wouldn't expect to see on such a derelict planet.

There were spotlights coming from the city, shining up and lighting up the dark skies. The city itself looks just as it had appeared from space; golden.

There are golden buildings, different coloured lights blinking on and off, making everything so bright.

Up in the sky, Mr Thinkalot notices the flying vehicles; oddly, some look just like the cars on Earth, except they are flying.

As he carries on watching, hypnotised by everything he sees, a sudden deafening siren screeches in his ears and from above, a bright, blinding light shines down on him.

Looking up, he spies a vehicle hovering above him with sirens and lights. Mr Thinkalot panics and starts to run away. The vehicle chases him and very soon catches up to Mr Thinkalot. He knows he can't run much further; he has been caught.

Putting his hands up in the air he shouts, "I give up."

The vehicle doesn't move. It just hovers high above him. Mr Thinkalot is scared; what will happen next? He waits. And then he watches on as two large, extendable, metal arms come from the vehicle and

grab hold of him tightly around his waist. Mr Thinkalot feels a sudden jolting movement as he sees a big, strong figure jump from the vehicle. The big, strong figure is attached to the large extendable arms holding Mr Thinkalot tight.

The figure thuds to the ground and runs at Mr Thinkalot with such speed. As it runs, the arms start to shrink as it gets closer until they are normal size and the figure stands right in right in front of its captive.

Struggling in the grasp of the figure's arms, Mr Thinkalot asks, "who are you?"

"I AM AN OFFICER OF THE ROBOT POLICE FORCE. MY NAME IS RPC MIKE AND YOU ARE UNDER ARREST."

?
?
RP
MIKE
RP

CHAPTER 5

"Why are you arresting me? "asks Mr Thinkalot.

"YOU FELL FROM OUR SKY WITHOUT ANY WARNING OR PERMISSION. YOU DID NOT ASK US IF IT WAS OK TO FALL FROM OUR SKY, THEREFORE YOU ARE AN UNIDENTIFIED FLYING OBJECT. WELL ACTUALLY, YOU ARE AN UNIDENTIFIED FALLING OBJECT BUT WE WON'T SPLIT ATOMS. ALL UFOS MUST BE INVESTIGATED, SO WE MUST DETAIN AND QUESTION YOU. I MUST TAKE YOU TO OUR LEADER!" RPC Mike says.

"Unidentified falling object? Ridiculous. My landing was perfectly fine thank you very much," mumbled Mr Thinkalot.

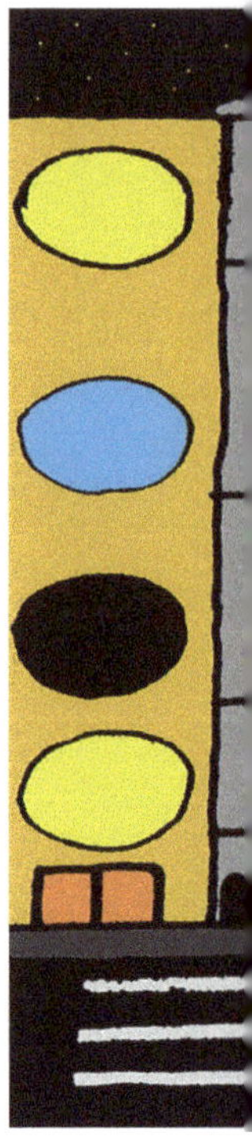

RPC Mike suddenly raises Mr Thinkalot above his head and starts to run fast and, in no time at all, he is running at 230 miles per hour. It's a good job that Mr Thinkalot has his **SUPER SPACE HELMET** on still or his face would be all flippy floppy!

Mr Thinkalot shouts, "Please slow down. Why are you running with me? Why didn't you take me in your police vehicle?"

"IT RAN OUT OF POWER - WE MUST GO ON FOOT."

"What is your planet called?" asks Mr Thinkalot.

"BOO BOO BEEP BEEP, YOU ARE UNDER ARREST, YOU ARE A UFO," RPC Mike repeats over and over again.

Mr Thinkalot realises he is going to get very little sense at all from RPC Mike, so he stops listening.

Finally, they arrive at the golden city, coming to a very abrupt and jerky stop. Mr Thinkalot is plonked on the roadside of the colourful, vibrant city. "How rude," he exclaims.

As he looks around at all the golden buildings, he thinks it could very easily be a city anywhere on Earth. Looking more closely, Mr Thinkalot can see clear tubes running up the side of each building and

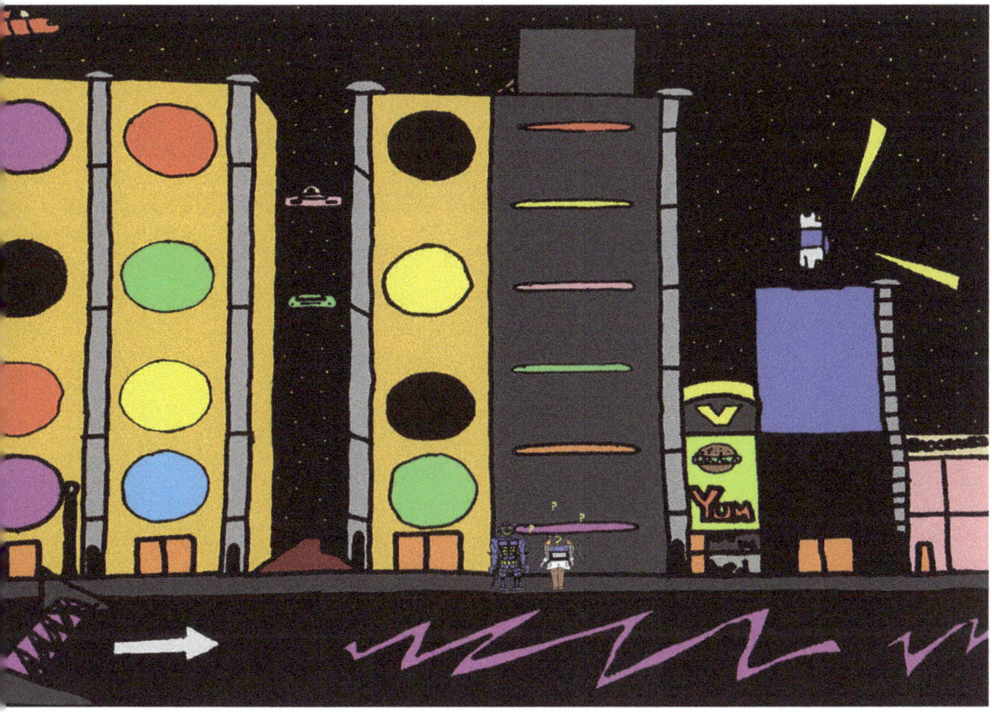

wonders what they might be. Then he spots more flying cars, "Wow unbelievable," he comments.

RPC Mike pulls Mr Thinkalot from his daze, "WE MUST GO TO THE LEADER AT ROBOT POLICE HEADQUARTERS." Handcuffing Mr Thinkalot to his robotty wrist, he drags him along the street like a criminal.

When they arrive at the RP HQ, RPC Mike pushes Mr Thinkalot through a door into one of the tubes running up the side of the building. As they are now attached at the wrist, RPC Mike joins him in the tube. They stand for a second and then there's a woosh as they get sucked up the tube to the top floor of the building.

“So that’s what these tubes are for. Now this is what I call fun,” Mr Thinkalot babbles.

As the tube stops, the door opens, RPC Mike takes Mr Thinkalot into the big open office. He unlocks the handcuff off his robot arm and handcuffs Mr Thinkalot to the desk. “WAIT HERE FOR OUR LEADER. HE WILL BE HERE SHORTLY TO INTERROGATE YOU.”

Mr Thinkalot panics as lots of different thoughts rush through his mind. He has so many theories to talk about and questions to ask.

Mr Thinkalot waits patiently, drumming the fingers of his uncuffed hand on the desk.

Looking around he can see lots of other rooms but no other beings, other than RPC Mike. Then he spots the interrogation room. He knows it’s the interrogation room because it has a sign on it saying, ‘Interrogation Room’.

“How odd,” he thinks, *“it’s written in English.”*

Outside the interrogation room, in a large brown pot, is a very strange looking plant. It has many tentacles and seven goggly eyes, all of which are watching Mr Thinkalot's every move. It's making Mr Thinkalot very nervous. He wonders if it's a security plant.

As well as drumming his fingers on the desk, Mr Thinkalot is now tapping his foot anxiously.

RPC Mike begins to make a strange sound from his desk and shouts loudly, "LEADER TO UFO INTERROGATION PLEASE."

Then heavy footsteps start coming along the corridor towards Mr Thinkalot.

"Whatever it is, it's coming and it's coming for me!" he shuddered.

ROBOT POLICE OFFICER
OF THE MONTH
MIKE WELL DONE
RP
R.P.D
INTERROGATION ROOM

CHAPTER 6

RPC Mike un-cuffs Mr Thinkalot from the desk and tells him to go to the interrogation room.

Mr Thinkalot races down the corridor towards the room and he comes to a sudden stop. His eyes nearly pop right out of his head! The leader is stood right there in front of him and is human - just like a man from Earth.

"I was not expecting this!" Mr Thinkalot says a bit louder than he intended.

The leader opens the interrogation room door and they both walk in. Inside there is a desk with a chair on either side.

The leader tells Mr Thinkalot to sit down and then joins him on the opposite side of the table. With so many questions racing around his brain Mr Thinkalot starts to sweat heavily, he bursts out, "Sir, are you human?"

"I am not here to answer your questions; you are here to answer mine. You are a UFO; you fell from our skies?"

"Yes, I suppose you could call me that," answers Mr Thinkalot.

"What are you and where are you from?"

"I am a human from planet Earth."

"Where is this planet Earth, we know of no such planet. And why have you come here?"

"Well, I'm a professor of science, I have a thirst to learn as much as I can. I want to question what I don't understand. I have so many questions I would like answers to."

"And what is this device on your head?"

"This is my **SUPER SPACE HELMET**. I designed it to go further into my solar system so I can test my theories and learn new things."

"So, you're here for educational reasons only?"

"Yes," Mr Thinkalot agrees.

"Well, I'm sorry but we must confiscate your **SUPER SPACE HELMET** so we can analyse it." The leader stretches his arms out to take it.

"No," Mr Thinkalot argues, "this is mine, I made it and it's my only way home."

"Mr Thinkalot I am trying to help you; I don't want RPC Mike to throw you in prison. You must understand that we have never had a visitor from another planet before, so we must make sure you are genuine and who you say you are. We need to check that you don't have any weapons or anything else that can harm us."

"But I come in peace," he replies. "How will I breath? Your oxygen levels are so low here?"

"Calm down, Mr Thinkalot. Our city has an invisible force field around it. It keeps the atmospheric oxygen levels at the right level so we can all breathe. We produce and recycle the oxygen you know," the leader tells him rather smugly, "as well as the gravity to stop us floating off into space. Beyond the city you would get into trouble."

Mr Thinkalot is both interested to learn about this planet but also worried.

"We will return your **SUPER SPACE HELMET** once we know it's safe. Now, you must be tired after your very long space journey so you can rest soon." The leader takes Mr Thinkalot's helmet off his head to send it away for inspection.

Mr Thinkalot takes in his first breath of alien air. He is amazed. It is **THE** freshest air he could have imagined, so clean and cool.

"Why would you risk your life, flying through space into the unknown just to learn?"

"I want to explore the unknown and help my planet. We need to find better ways to progress and evolve, to ensure our planet's survival. What do you call your world? What is it like outside the city?" Mr Thinkalot asks.

"Our planet is called Eden," replies the leader.

Before he could continue, an alarm sounds. "I'm sorry Mr Thinkalot, your time's up – no more questions. I have compiled your file with your statement and it will soon be time for you to see the Council of Three."

"The Council of Three? What is that?" Mr Thinkalot asks, trying not to panic.

"My job was to get to know you a little bit, find out about you. When you have rested, the Council of Three will interrogate you."

"Interrogate me; No, not again," he says, "I come in peace."

"Yes Mr Thinkalot, the Council will decide your fate. The Council of Three know you have arrived; ***THEY*** are the ones you have to convince!

You will not actually be able to see them though as they will wear cloaking devices to conceal and protect their identities. They are a very private species and they only reveal themselves if they trust you.

Please listen to the council Mr Thinkalot. You don't want to make them angry. Just listen to their questions and answer truthfully. They have the power to send you back home, or worse still, to prison; and believe me, you don't want to go there," the leader explained.

The leader hands Mr Thinkalot a key with the words 'sleeping quarters' on it. "Come with me and I'll show you your quarters."

They leave the interrogation room together and walk up the corridor to the sleeping quarters door.

"This is your room, rest and be ready for the council when you wake."

The leader shakes Mr Thinkalot's hand and wishes him good luck and walks quickly off back down the corridor.

SLEEEPING
QUARTERS

CHAPTER 7

Mr Thinkalot unlocks the door with the key, and walks in. It's a clean, white box of a room. It's bright but there are no windows and no lights that he can see. Nor is there any furniture; absolutely nothing in it.

"Well isn't this odd! What on Eden am I supposed to sleep on?" Mr Thinkalot muses.

As he looks around the room, he sees a circle on the floor. He steps into the circle and as soon as he does, a glowing orb like light rises out the floor and floats above him. Mr Thinkalot tries to touch the orb but as he does, a pleasant voice echoes out across the room, "WELCOME MR THINKALOT, HOW ARE YOU TODAY?"

"Who are you?"

"I AM YOUR SLEEPING QUARTERS' PERSONAL ASSISTANT, I'M HERE TO ASSIST YOU WITH ANYTHING YOU NEED TO MAKE YOUR STAY AS COMFORTABLE AS POSSIBLE. IS THERE ANYTHING I CAN DO FOR YOU?" the voice asks.

"Do you have a name?"

"A NAME? WHY WOULD I NEED A NAME?"

"Well I can't keep calling you sleeping quarters personal assistant can I! So, I shall call you Paisley if that's OK."

"AS YOU WISH MR THINKALOT."

"I am hungry," he says rubbing his stomach, "could I have a jacket potato please?"

A beautiful harp like noise fills the room, then right before his very eyes, a table and chair appear in the middle of the room. Next, a plate appears on the table with a steaming hot, green jacket potato. Mr Thinkalot stands there all confused, massaging his beard between his fingertips.

"How is this possible?" he exclaims "amazing, just amazing."

He walks over to the table and looks at the peculiar potato.

"Why is it green?"

Paisley replies, "WHAT COLOUR DID YOU EXPECT IT TO BE? THIS IS THE COLOUR THEY ARE ON EDEN."

He puts his nose near the green jacket potato and gives it an almighty big sniff.

"Mmm smells like an Earth jacket potato, could I have a knife and fork please" he asks.

The beautiful harp like noise fills the room again, then the cutlery magically appears before his very eyes; he wastes no time in tucking in, now realising he is really hungry. He chomps away at the potato.

A full Mr Thinkalot stands up and walks away from the table. The table breaks down into thousands of little pieces, before disappearing completely.

"I am rather sleepy now, could I have a bed to sleep on please Paisley?" he says. The harp sound fills the room again and a bed appears in the centre of the room. "perfect, thank you. You're an absolute star, this bed looks fantastic."

"I AM NOT A STAR MR THINKALOT, I HAVE ALREADY EXPLAINED I AM A PERSONAL ASSISTANT. ARE ALL EARTH PEOPLE AS STRANGE AS YOU?" Paisley asks quite quietly.

Mr Thinkalot hops onto the bed. He's not sure he is going to be able to sleep though as his mind is so full of busy thoughts.

He asks Paisley, "Would it be possible for me to have a hot chocolate beverage?"

The harp music comes again and hey presto, next to the bed a small side table appears with a lovely big mug of frothy hot chocolate.

"Marvellous, a room that grants wishes; I need to invent this," he jokes.

Mr Thinkalot lets out a big yawn, as his eyes slowly close he nods off to sleep. He dreams of his fantastic space journey and his achievements.

Within minutes, a loud alarm goes off. Mr Thinkalot awakes with a start and falls out of bed.

From his new place on the floor, he asks, "what the... what was that?"

Paisley speaks, "I HAVE FAST FORWARDED YOUR SLEEP CYCLE. YOU HAVE HAD MAXIMUM REST MR THINKALOT AND ARE NOW FULLY REFRESHED AND ENERGISED TO GO."

Mr Thinkalot realises he's full of energy and feels very refreshed. "Unbelievable," he comments.

"THE COUNCIL OF THREE IS GETTING READY FOR YOU MR THINKALOT; IT'S TIME TO GET READY FOR YOUR INTERROGATION. WOULD YOU LIKE A SHOWER?"

"That would be brilliant thank you Paisley," he answers.

Suddenly, two circular metallic orbs appear from out of the floor and head towards Mr Thinkalot. They chase him around the room, until he realises they are the Eden version of a shower; one orb washing and the other drying. A toothbrush appears and wriggles into his mouth and starts brushing his teeth at the same time. By the time the shower orbs are finished, he is super fresh and his clothes clean and dry. *"Oh, this is just incredible. I can see that I need to invent these at home too. How much power and water they could save!"* Mr Thinkalot thinks to himself.

Paisley calls out, "MR THINKALOT THE COUNCIL OF THREE IS READY TO SEE YOU, PLEASE MAKE YOUR WAY TO THE INTERROGATION ROOM FOR INTERROGATION. THANK YOU FOR CHOOSING TO STAY AT THE SLEEPING QUARTERS, I HOPE YOU ENJOYED YOUR STAY WITH US."

"Thank you, Paisley the PA," says Mr Thinkalot as he makes his way out of the room and down the corridor.

CHAPTER 8

Mr Thinkalot makes his way to the interrogation room; the door opens automatically but there is no one in the room. He sits down on a chair in front of the desk and waits patiently.

The room's lights dim making it very difficult to see anything.

All of a sudden, a disembodied voice announces, "THE COUNCIL HAS ARRIVED."

Mr Thinkalot hears the door open, and something enters the room making a weird splish, splash, splosh noise. He tries to think what the noise reminds him of and it dawns on him that it sounds like someone walking through a huge puddle.

Then a second something comes into the room but the noise that this something makes is very different to the first something. This is more like a slithering, scraping and scratching sound all rolled into one. Mr Thinkalot can't think of anything that reminds him of this at all and to be perfectly honest, he is really not looking forward to seeing what is making that noise!

Mr Thinkalot is absolutely dreading what the third something is going to sound like. But the third something doesn't really make a noise as such, it's just a big gust of wind across his face. "I'm not sure

I'd prefer this one with a noise or not," thinks Mr Thinkalot.

There is no noise for about 10 seconds. All the splish, splash, sploshing, the slithering, scraping, scratching and the wind gusting has stopped. It's like a vacuum and Mr Thinkalot hardly dares breathe.

Suddenly, three voices all spoke at exactly the same time, "we are the Council of Three Mr Thinkalot and we are here to determine your fate. We apologise that we must use cloaking devices, but we must protect our identities as we do not know you, or that we can trust you. We will determine if you are telling the truth or not and your answers will be closely scrutinised."

Mr Thinkalot sits there patiently waiting for the questions, remembering what the leader had advised.

"We have been through your file completed by the leader and we have already read your statement. So, we will begin. Who are you?"

Thinking the council sound like some sort of alien boy band speaking totally in sync, Mr Thinkalot answers, "I am a human and my name is Mr Thinkalot."

"Why are you here?"

"I am a professor of science, I am here purely for educational purposes, to understand more, learn more and hopefully to help humanity achieve its greatest potential."

"Will you, your home world or any of its citizens cause our planet harm?".

"No, no, no. I come in peace. I would never deceive you."

"Can we trust you, Mr Thinkalot?"

"Yes, I mean you know harm. I just want to learn from you."

"Have you been telling us the truth?" they ask.

Mr Thinkalot just gives a simple yes to the Council of Three.

"We will now discuss your future."

Mr Thinkalot holds on tight to his chair, as he hears the three beings scuttle off to the back of the room. He hears three different voices but can't think which voice belongs to which sound they made when they came into the interrogation room. He can't decide which voice would fit a splish, splash, splosh, a slither, scrape, scratch or a bit of wind! Maybe they have voice changers he thinks to himself. He can't understand a word they are saying either. It is all quite frustrating, sitting in almost total darkness, not knowing what is being said about him.

All of a sudden, the room lights up. As Mr Thinkalot's eyes adjust to the brightness, he discovers that the

Council of Three have disappeared. "How on Earth did they do that?" he wonders again to himself.

Mr Thinkalot suddenly realises that the leader is now in the room with him. "And how did he do that?" he mutters under his breath.

"Congratulations Mr Thinkalot, the Council of Three have made their decision. They have granted you permission to stay so that you can learn our ways. Time is of the essence; you will not have long here as time is precious to us and we have much to do.

I will be your guide. Meet me at RPC Mike's desk to collect your ***SUPER SPACE HELMET***, and we will be on our way."

"Thank you ever so much," Mr Thinkalot replies very excitedly.

He jumps off his chair with eagerness and anticipation to learn and ask questions; his thoughts racing through his brain as he makes his way to RPC Mike's desk.

CHAPTER 9

Mr Thinkalot waits for a short while for the leader.

He arrives with a big cheesy grin on his face and shakes Mr Thinkalot's hand, saying, "well done, I'm glad you could stay. I told you I was on your side. Here is your ***SUPER SPACE HELMET*** as promised."

Mr Thinkalot places the helmet over his head, as the leader places a breathing helmet over his head. "Are you ready for an adventure? Let's get on with the tour of the planet."

"Oh yes, I am more than ready."

"Are you ready to teleport?" the leader asks.

"Teleportation, are you kidding me? Teleport where?" he asks, hardly able to contain his excitement, "I've not done this before."

"We are going to teleport back onto the street of the golden city." The leader activates a button on his belt and a green circle opens up on the floor.

Mr Thinkalot wastes no time and jumps onto the green circle and with a flash he is back outside on the street. Another green circle opens up on the ground next to him and the leader appears.

"That was amazing," Mr Thinkalot shouts, "how was that possible?"

"Unfortunately, there isn't the time to explain; we must move on with the tour. So much to see and so little time," the leader replies while looking up in the air, "any minute now."

Mr Thinkalot looks up too and notices some kind of energy field. Then out of the energy, what looks to be a floating bus appears and slowly drifts to the ground right in front of them.

The door opens automatically and the leader escorts Mr Thinkalot onto the bus.

"Why is there no driver?" Mr Thinkalot asks in a bit of panic.

"Oh, it's automated, no need for a driver. The bus is already programmed with the directions."

Then a bell sounds from the front of the bus and a voice announces, "WELCOME ON BOARD THE EDEN GALACTIC BUS SERVICE. FIRST STOP THE POWER PLANT SECTOR. PLEASE FASTEN YOUR SEAT BELTS AND ENJOY THE JOURNEY."

Mr Thinkalot and the leader both find a seat, sit down and fasten their seat belts.

Then there's another announcement, "INITIATING JOURNEY."

"Hang on tight," advises the leader.

Suddenly, the bus jolts backwards on its behind. It was a bit like being on the upward part of a rollercoaster. Mr Thinkalot's and the leader's legs dangle off the edge of their seats; not really very comfortable. Out of the window they could see they were aiming up to the dark alien space above Eden.

"COMMENCING COUNTDOWN," the bus announces, "5,4,3,2,1."

The engines engage with a mighty roar and the bus is off, rocketing into the sky high above the city. As they reach higher altitude, the bus begins to straighten off, and feeling a bit more at ease, Mr Thinkalot thinks it's a perfect time to ask questions.

"Where are all your inhabitants? I haven't seen anyone other than you, the Council of Three and RPC Mike?"

"Mr Thinkalot, our planet is on lockdown, and our citizens are too scared to come outside. The oxygen level outside of the city is very low for much of the time. If there's not enough air everyone must stay indoors.

Of course, the other reason you haven't seen anybody is that everyone is a bit worried about you being here. You have to understand, we have never had a visitor on Eden before.

But let's not concentrate on that right now, you convinced the council that it is safe to have you here and that's all that matters."

Mr Thinkalot nods to show his understanding; he would feel exactly the same if aliens came to Earth – most people would hide. But not Mr Thinkalot; he'd want to be one of the welcoming party.

As he looks out of the window, he points at a large building, "what's that down there?"

The leader responds with, "oh yes that's our All About Eden shopping centre; you can get anything from there, absolutely anything."

"And what are they, those floating machines?" asks Mr Thinkalot, pointing in another direction.

"Oh, they're our nanobots. They do all our manual work – they are our builders."

The bus slows down and comes to a stop in mid-air. Then it falls down to the ground at a rapid speed. Mr Thinkalot is panicking and just then, the bus announces, "NEXT STOP POWER PLANT."

The bus carries on falling till it's half a meter off the ground and then it stops dead.

"Are we still alive?"

The leader chuckles, "yes we are."

They unfasten their seatbelts, stand up and jump off the bus.

The bus announces, "THANK YOU FOR TRAVELLING ON THE EDEN GALACTIC BUS SERVICE."

"Your planet is pretty cool," Mr Thinkalot says to the leader.

"It was," replies the leader sadly. "We have arrived at the Power Plant Sector; let's go."

CHAPTER 10

They walk for a few seconds before Mr Thinkalot spots the power plant sector. Just next to the plant are loads of solar panels stretching across the red landscape. To Mr Thinkalot it looks breath taking.

The leader asks, "What do you think?"

"We have solar panels and power plants on our planet," Mr Thinkalot replies.

"Oh really, what kind of power do you use to fuel them?"

"We use all types of fuel; gas, coal, oil, and some use nuclear."

Before Mr Thinkalot can say anything else, the leader interrupts (quite rudely really), "So, you are using up all your planet's natural resources?"

"Well, yes, we do seem to be doing that," Mr Thinkalot responds thoughtfully.

"Well maybe you could start looking at using planet friendly methods rather than eat up its natural resources. There is no reason to push your planet to the brink of destruction is there!" the leader advised sagely.

"We are trying to improve but some people are very set in their ways and don't want to try."

"Oh, well it's great that you are at least trying."

They walk closer to the power plant and the leader explains "All the air for the city is created here. It's then pumped out, comes back, is purified and pumped out again. We also store the energy from the sun with all of these solar panels to power the city and its vehicles. If we run low on energy, the city becomes a dark place and the flying vehicles may stop in mid-air until energy is restored."

They walk away from the power plant sector and head towards what appeared to be traffic lights by a damaged road. The button on the traffic lights reads **'FLUID TRAVEL'.**

Mr Thinkalot asks, "What on Eden is fluid travel?"

"If you press the button it will take us to our next location."

"How interesting," Mr Thinkalot thinks, wondering what the button will do. Unable to resist, he presses the button.

Immediately, Mr Thinkalot almost regrets pressing the button as an energy beam zips out from the traffic light thing and zaps them both. They are both fizzing with power and Mr Thinkalot thinks, *"it's like I've eaten five bowls of brekkie."*

He asks, "Hold on, what is this? Are we electric?"

The leader nods.

"Fantastic. Amazing."

The leader prods Mr Thinkalot and announces, "Now we are ready. Come on, let's use that power!" They set off running and in no time at all they have covered a few miles.

Zig zagging all over the place, they pass ruins of an old city, the houses now rubble and dust. Mr Thinkalot is really enjoying seeing everything speed past. Bert is obviously not quite as happy, as he can be heard BEEP BOPPING in low tones in the SUPER SPACE HELMET and Mr Thinkalot thinks he hears Bert say in a very low monotone tone, "THIS IS MAKING MY CIRCUITS HURT."

"Where are we going Leader?"

"We are going to Eden Beach."

"Oh wonderful. I love going to the beach and having a paddle in the sea," exclaims Mr Thinkalot excitedly, "I bet it's really beautiful and full of tropical palm trees and things."

Gradually they slow down to a walking pace.

Bert can be heard muttering, "THANK GOODNESS FOR THAT. I THOUGHT MY HARD DRIVE WAS GOING TO MELT."

The two men start to walk and follow damaged, rusty signs to the glorious Eden beach. They arrive and Mr Thinkalot's mouth drops wide open. What he sees is not at all what he expected. There is no beach. There is no golden sand and clear blue sea. Instead, in front of them is a red dust wasteland. There is a boat wreck and a rotten old animal skull.

"Where's the beach?" Mr Thinkalot asks the leader.

"We have no beach or seas now. This was once the most beautiful beach and the seas were full of life."

"What happened?"

The leader tells Mr Thinkalot the tale of what had happened to Eden, explaining that through years of overfishing, dumping toxic materials like plastic in the seas, the vital eco system was destroyed. There were Eden quakes and tsunamis, the atmosphere virtually disappeared, meaning that the seas dried up and all wildlife died. The leader sheds a tear as he tells the tale.

"Do you have wildlife on your planet, Mr Thinkalot?"

Then Mr Thinkalot replies telling the story of planet Earth and describing the wonderful wildlife that exists and those species that are in danger.

The leader's eyes open wide with astonishment as he listens about tigers and whales, polar bears and orangutans, eagles and penguins, and all the wonderful places they live in. But the leader's face changes to one of sadness when he hears how some of those wonderful animals and forests are being destroyed.

"Life is so very precious Mr Thinkalot. Your people should do more to protect the planet before it's too late. What would be the point if everything you had ever worked for as a species is lost and your beautiful world is destroyed?"

The leader shakes his head and continues, "Our races are very much alike you know. We polluted our air, chopped down all our trees, mined all our planet's natural resources. We over farmed the land so that our soil would no longer grow anything."

The leader was really very sad now, "I would hate for your world to suffer from the same catastrophic events that we have caused to ours. Do you think you could convince your people to work together to stop destroying everything?"

Mr Thinkalot, rubbing his beard thoughtfully, is still listening to the leader as he carries on talking.

"You probably don't know but you have to think fast when the end of the world is coming. We built our force field first, so that the air we produce at the plant can be pumped into the city, caught and then recycled to be used again.

Then we had to collect what other natural resources were left which, to be honest, was not much. There was only 10% of our good soil and fresh water left. We had to develop ways to minimise usage and recycle everything. We analysed the soil we saved and were able to create a synthetic version and, although it's not as good, we do get some growth from it.

Could your inhabitants adapt so quickly if you knew your planet was dying?"

Shaking his head as he thinks about humans' flaws and what could happen if things don't change, Mr Thinkalot replies, "No, I don't believe we could. But your technology is so much more advanced than ours and you have survived; isn't that something to celebrate?"

The leader becomes a bit cross, "our once beautiful planet is now a wasteland. We struggle to grow enough food to feed all the inhabitants, there are no animals left and hardly any water. Open your eyes; your planet is on the same path of destruction."

Mr Thinkalot hangs his head in shame, "I am sorry, please accept my apology. I can see you are trying to teach me so I can help my own planet."

The leader smiles as he forgives Mr Thinkalot. "When you're living on borrowed time, everyone needs to do their bit, but it's usually the leaders who need to work together. Do you think your leaders will be able to do this to save your planet before it's too late?"

Mr Thinkalot says with sudden confidence and positivity, "I'm going to fight with all my might for change."

"And do you think they will listen to just one man?"

"Ha," Mr Thinkalot replies, "this one man came this far, the furthest any of our race has ever been. No one believed I could do that, so I have to believe, that I, Mr Thinkalot, can do this and make them listen to me."

CHAPTER 11

After their discussion the leader points way out in the distance, "can you see that over there Mr Thinkalot?"

"What is it?

"It's our farming facilities and that's the next place we are going to visit." The leader continues, "you know Mr Thinkalot, it's been really nice getting to know you and to learn about your planet and species."

"Honestly, thank you for showing me everything. It is all so fascinating and sad at the same time."

They start to walk down a path towards the fluid travel traffic light system. The leader presses the button, the traffic light zaps them with its energy beam again and the pair fizz like they did before. They start running really fast - like bolts of lightning.

From the depths of the SUPER SPACE HELMET, Bert sighs, "OH NOT AGAIN!"

The leader and Mr Thinkalot race past more derelict land, demolished houses, decayed forests; a very sad sight.

"Are you hungry Mr Thinkalot?"

"Indeed I am."

"Come on then, follow me; I know just the place."

Zooming along, they run back to the golden city and head straight to Yum's Restaurant. They come to a stop, open the door and go in.

The diner is empty, so they pick the best table, plop down onto the seats and remove their helmets, putting them carefully on the floor next to their feet.

Mr Thinkalot thought he heard Bert burp but shakes his head thinking he's just hearing things.

The leader passes Mr Thinkalot the menu and they decide what to eat. A loud crashing noise comes from the back of the diner, as a voice shouts, "I'LL BE RIGHT OUT."

A beautiful woman appears from the kitchen and stands behind the counter. "I'LL COME TO TAKE YOUR ORDERS IN ONE SECOND," she says. Mr Thinkalot's face goes a bright shade of red as he blushes at the lady. The leader starts to chuckle, "are you okay Mr Thinkalot?"

Flustered, Mr Thinkalot mumbles something about being 'fine' and drops his menu on the floor. He leans down to pick it up and looks across at the lady again. As she comes from behind the counter to take their orders, he sees that where she should have legs and feet, she has a wheel. She screeches and skids her way to their table.

Then it dawns on Mr Thinkalot. “Wait, wait - what!” he chortles as he realises the waitress is not a human; she is a robot. From the waist up she looks so human and life like with long flowing hair. And she is so pretty. But she is balancing, in a wobbly sort of way, on one wheel next to their table.

“HI, I’M MAGGIE, WHAT CAN I GET YOU?” she asks.

Mr Thinkalot is so shocked that his eyes and mouth are wide open.

The leader dives right in and asks, “Hi Maggie, I would love one of your cheesy broccoli cauliflower burgers please.”

Maggie acknowledges the leader, “YOU WANT VEGETABLE FRIES WITH THAT?”

“Oh no, that will be all for me Maggie, thank you.”

“AND WHAT CAN I GET YOU SIR?” she asks looking at Mr Thinkalot.

He panics and on impulse asks, “Could I have a spicy bean burger please?”

“DO YOU WANT ANY VEGETABLE FRIES TO GO WITH THAT?” Maggie asks.

“No, that’s great for me thank you.”

“ANY DRINKS WITH YOUR BURGERS?” They both shake their heads.

Maggie does a wheelie and heads into the kitchen.

Mr Thinkalot can't help but watch as she cooks and prepares the burgers. She is an absolute whizz in the kitchen, moving so fast, flipping a burger with each hand. Mr Thinkalot's stomach starts to rumble as the smell of the cooking food reaches his nose.

In a rather deep voice, Mr Thinkalot comments, "she's a master chef."

In no time at all Maggie wheels herself back to their table, "ONE SPICY BEAN BURGER NO FRIES; ONE CHEESY BROCCOLI CAULIFLOWER BURGER NO FRIES," she says, placing the delicious smelling vegetable burgers on the table.

Mr Thinkalot picks up his burger with both hands and takes a huge bite. What a mistake! He jumps off his chair like a rocket, yelling, "ooooooww it's **SO HOT**." His mouth feels like it is on fire.

Maggie rolls back to the table, "IS EVERYTHING OKAY?"

"What is in this burger?"

Maggie lists the ingredients, "A VARIETY OF BEANS WITH CHILLI. DID YOU NOT READ THE MENU?"

Mr Thinkalot replies, "I like chilli but not that much; I'm sorry."

Maggie takes the burger and holds it in her hands. Then, she closes her eyes for a couple of seconds. "I HAVE REMOVED THE CHILLI."

Mr Thinkalot is a bit confused, "but how, you only held the burger in your hands."

"WE DO NOT TOLERATE WASTE HERE," she says. "I WAS DESIGNED TO REMOVE INGREDIENTS JUST BY HOLDING THE FOOD AND CLOSING MY EYES. IT THEN GOES INTO MY WASTE TRAY AND IS RECYCLED AS FERTILISER FOR THE SOIL. ANYWAY, TRY IT NOW, SEE IF IT TASTES BETTER."

Mr Thinkalot takes another bite of his burger and it is full of chilli free deliciousness. "Oh, thank you Maggie; perfect," he says with a full mouth.

Suddenly, the restaurant door swings open and two cloud like figures come in. They float into the diner, in a cloudy sort of way, and drift towards a table and float down onto the seats. Maggie wheels over and takes their order for veggie burgers.

Mr Thinkalot wonders how cloudy beings like them can eat anything at all but asks, "what are they?"

"Oh, that's two of the Council of Three. They are in disguise."

"Where's number three then?"

"I don't know," replies the leader, "perhaps he is just not hungry today."

Mr Thinkalot feels ever so slightly that he is being spied on.

The leader finishes his burger and tells Mr Thinkalot that when they've both finished, they need to get off to their next location.

Mr Thinkalot keeps taking bites from his chilli free burger. "This is delicious, **CHOMP**. These are not just yum, **CHOMP**, burgers - they are yum yum burgers. **CHOMP**."

When he has finished, he stands up, puts on his **SUPER SPACE HELMET** and heads towards the door. As he does, there's a screeching, skidding noise coming from the kitchen. He turns to see if the leader is also ready to leave but in front of him is a finger wagging Maggie!

"HEY. YOU NEED TO PUT YOUR PACKAGING INTO THE RECYCLING BIN BEFORE YOU LEAVE SIR."

"Oh, sorry Maggie. I didn't know that; I've never been here before."

Maggie shouts, "IT DOESN'T MATTER WHERE YOU'RE FROM, YOU SHOULD ALWAYS RECYCLE."

"You are absolutely right Maggie." Mr Thinkalot picks up his rubbish and puts it in the recycling bin.

The leader smiles, stands up and puts his helmet on ready to carry on with the tour.

As they leave the diner, they both shout, "thank you Maggie, your food is delicious."

Maggie wheels out of the kitchen and replies, "THANK YOU FOR EATING AT YUM, THE BEST BURGER JOINT IN THE GALAXY. YOU'RE WELCOME BACK ANYTIME."

From their table, the two cloudy council members eat their burgers and whisper to each other as they watch the leader and Mr Thinkalot leave.

CHAPTER 12

The leader and Mr Thinkalot walk to the fluid travel traffic light system. This time, Mr Thinkalot presses the button and the beam zaps them, filling them with energy. He is still not sure how he feels about being zapped but is almost getting used to it. Almost.

Zooming off towards their next destination, they pass more destruction and wasteland. It makes them both look very sad beneath their helmets and makes Mr Thinkalot think more about making sure this doesn't happen at home.

"So, here we are at the farming station," the leader says as they arrive. There are floating greenhouses, full of lovely vegetables and fruit.

The leader carries on explaining about the farm. "I have already explained how we lost the majority of our resources, so I won't bore you with all the details again. We have to do everything efficiently with no mistakes. We have to make sure there is enough air, soil and water for the plants to grow. Each greenhouse is filled to an exact, efficient capacity.

Nothing is wasted; everything is used and now our crops grow better than they ever did before."

Mr Thinkalot asks, So why do the greenhouses float in the air?"

"They rotate so that each plant, vegetable and fruit has the perfect amount of sunlight to grow perfectly.

We can grow any vegetable and fruit; there's nothing we can't grow. We have created the perfect climate to grow anything, even in the same greenhouse.

The greenhouses float as we pump the air directly up into them from underneath. That's what makes them float. And the way the air is pumped makes them rotate in a full circle. It's all done with the least resources and effort needed. Even better, we don't need any pesticides – everything is completely organic and there is no waste.

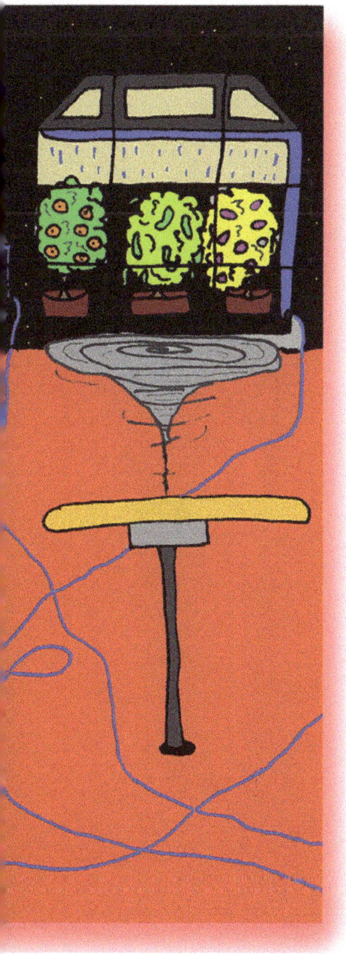

I am really pleased we were able to come up with such an innovative way of doing things. We are lucky that we can feed all of the inhabitants."

Rubbing his beard again, Mr Thinkalot understands exactly how it works, it all makes perfect sense. He is really very impressed and adds, "this is such a clever little system, so simple. I hope we may be able to replicate this back on Earth. Who looks after all the plants?"

"If we wait a few more moments we will see the gardeners in action," the leader replies. "They are very efficient. Plus, we have a large underground storage area to keep all the food in. That keeps it fresh, so it doesn't go off quickly."

As they wait for the gardeners' arrival, Mr Thinkalot stares at the farm, amazed at how well they have adapted in such a crisis.

The leader looks at his watch and starts a countdown, "5,4,3,2,1. Here they come Mr Thinkalot – look."

A loud bell chimes and then lots of lights enter the greenhouses. Oddly, they seem to be maintaining the plants, picking the ripe fruit and vegetables, carrying them away and dropping them in a chute that leads to the underground storage facility.

The little lights flickering as they work is so lovely to watch. It's almost as if they have put on an amazing light show especially for them.

Mr Thinkalot squints his eyes to see if he can make them out what the lights are. “What are they?” he asks the leader.

“They're millions of mini robots. They work as one big team, helping to care for the plants, making sure every plant has the correct amount of air, water, heat and sunlight to grow the best produce. Then, when the plants are ready, they pick the fruit and veggies and put them in the storage unit. They really are the best gardeners you could ask for; they never let us down.”

Mr Thinkalot is in awe watching these beautiful little machines doing their fantastic jobs.

The leader looks at him and asks, “have you enjoyed your time here? I have had fun showing you around the planet.”

“It's been brilliant, I have enjoyed every second of it. Thank you for making me so welcome and showing me around.”

“Well, it is time to head back to the golden city, as our time is nearly up.”

“Oh, I wish I could stay here longer,” sighs Mr Thinkalot.

“You never know, we might see you again in the future Mr Thinkalot.”

“I do hope so,” he replies as they walk away from the farming facility.

Tele

CHAPTER 13

"How would you like to try something new Mr Thinkalot? Just down this broken road is a special Eden telephone box, which will allow us to teleport back to the golden city."

Mr Thinkalot is puzzled, "I thought you could only teleport short distances? That's what you said earlier."

"Well that was partly right as my belt teleporter will only allow us to travel short distances. We have to get back to the golden city soon but there's one more special place I would like to take you. There are telephone boxes scattered around the planet for the inhabitants to get to and from the city quickly."

"Okay, that sounds exciting. So, what is this special place you're taking me to?" Mr Thinkalot asks.

"You'll see when we get there," the leader responds knowingly.

They walk down the broken road and arrive at a telephone box. They squeeze into it – it's quite difficult for them both to fit and they jostle around so they can close the door. The leader puts his eye up to an eye scanner, picks up the receiver and whispers something into it. Then they, and the telephone box vanish.

Then they reappear, but they are not in the same place, and this place is awful and scary.

"Oh my! You have brought me to a war zone," Mr Thinkalot shouts.

The leader replies quietly, "Unfortunately, when the planet started to fail, the leaders of Eden and its countries, fought instead of working together. So many of the citizens were lost. If only they could have worked together as one species instead of fighting each other. I mean war – huh, what is it good for? Absolutely nothing. It's just a waste of resources."

Mr Thinkalot looks over the vast area and sees rusting tanks, helicopters and cannons. And bones. There are a lot of bones. It must have been a massive war. They both close their eyes and have a minute's silence for the fallen soldiers.

Mr Thinkalot groans, "why couldn't everyone just get along, what's the point in working against each other - surely it's better to work together?"

"I couldn't agree more Mr Thinkalot. All the money wasted on the war could have been used for projects to help our planet. Working together for peace is always better."

They walk slowly back to the telephone box. They both squeeze inside. The leader tells Mr Thinkalot to put his eye up to the eye scanner, lift up the telephone receiver and say, "golden city."

Then they, and the telephone box vanish; again.

This time they reappear in the city just across from the Robot Police Headquarters.

Mr Thinkalot says, “That was so cool”.

He spots Maggie waving to him from the diner. "BYE, BYE," she shouts. Mr Thinkalot gives her a wave back and beams at her. Then he joins the leader and they head into the tube lift up to the top floor of the police station.

"Mr Thinkalot, you go along to the interrogation room, there is a surprise waiting for you there, I will join you shortly." Mr Thinkalot heads to the interrogation room and opens the door. It's pitch black inside but he goes in.

All of a sudden, lots of voices shout out, "*SURPRISE.*" The lights come on and there, in front of him are RPC Mike, Maggie, and two of the cloudlike council members. It is a huge party for him. There is lots of music, food and drink.

Maggie rolls up to Mr Thinkalot and asks him to dance with her. They start dancing in the middle of the room and then the others join in too. RPC Mike does some robot dancing and the council members do a bit of floating together. Everyone is having a jolly good time, dancing around, joking and being silly.

The door opens and the leader walks in and everyone shouts for him to join in the fun. They all chatter, eat food and have some nice fruit smoothies.

Whilst talking to Mr Thinkalot, the leader muses, "I would like to thank you Mr Thinkalot, you are a true friend. I hope we can continue to be friends."

"Oh, I'd like that."

The leader walks to the back of the room and grabs a microphone to make a speech. The lights and music die down so the room is pitch black again.

The leader coughs to get everyone's attention.

"Mr Thinkalot, I have something I need to tell you; I haven't been 100% honest with you and for that I apologise. I think it's time I show you my true form. I had my reasons for not telling you the truth, I hope you can understand."

The lights come back on, and there - instead of the leader with his brown hair and moustache, wearing a suit with a golden sash - is someone else or rather something else. There in his place is a different being; he is green and blue with a distinctive amphibian look about him. And instead of two eyes, there is just one large blue eye in the middle of his forehead. The leader is a cyclops being.

"My name is actually Wave and I am from another planet in this solar system; a planet full of deep oceans called Gallons. I came here to try and help this devastated planet. I have worked hard and helped the Edenians achieve more than they could have done alone. But just like Earth and Eden, my home planet is also at a critical point so I may have to return home soon."

"Oh no, not another planet," Mr Thinkalot thinks to himself.

Wave comes over to Mr Thinkalot and says "I hope you can forgive me. I wasn't sure how you'd react to seeing someone like me. I needed to know I could trust you but I must admit I trusted you quickly. I soon knew you wouldn't be judgemental but I disguised myself just to make sure you felt comfortable with me."

Mr Thinkalot is standing there with his mouth wide open in surprise.

"I am also part of the council of three. I am sorry for deceiving you."

The other two cloudy council members start to clap; one with a slither, scrape, scratch and the other, a gusty windy sort of noise. They say in in sync, "maybe in the future when we can trust you, we may reveal ourselves to you also."

The room erupts with everyone cheering and clapping really loudly.

Maggie wheels over to Mr Thinkalot, "WHAT HAVE YOU LEARNED ON YOUR JOURNEY AND TIME ON EDEN?"

Mr Thinkalot rubs his beard then replies, "I have learned how important life and our planets are. We should stop using all their natural resources, recycle and not waste anything. We need to find safer, cleaner ways to do things and use our technology to make the worlds the best that they can be, not to destroy them."

Wave comments, "that's fantastic Mr Thinkalot but what else have you learned?"

"Oh, hhhmmmm, I'm not sure, have I missed something out?" asks Mr Thinkalot, rubbing his beard a bit more.

Wave whispers in his ear, "what about the vegetables and fruit?"

Mr Thinkalot looks confused and mutters very unconvincingly, "eerrrrmmmm, fruit and vegetables."

Wave interrupts, "you know your planet is in grave danger and that you must do something. You must show your people they have lost sight of what's important before it's too late."

Mr Thinkalot nods.

Wave continues, "what about the importance of fruits and vegetables?"

Mr Thinkalot starts to panic, "I don't know, I must have missed that part."

"What is the most important thing? The solution that holds the key in saving your planet?"

"Honestly, I don't know," Mr Thinkalot admits, slightly ashamed.

"It's all about working from the ground up. It's not just what you do to the planet, it's about what your people eat. The planet provides so many fruit and vegetables. They're not there for fun you know. They're there to feed the life on the planet?

Inside every fruit and vegetable are vitamins, minerals and fibre. These things all work to keep your body healthy and help it to heal itself. Some vitamins and minerals help your eyes, some your skin and hair and others can help keep your mind fit.

Just imagine if all your people ate lots of fruit and vegetables. They'd be stronger, healthier and fitter, with clearer, more positive minds. They would have the potential to explode with creativity and the ability to achieve more, and be able to work for a better, healthier planet.

You need to convince your people and get the adults to explain it to the children. Children are the future with the potential to be real heroes. They are the ones who can save your planet."

Slightly unconvinced, Mr Thinkalot asks, "really? I convince the children to eat better, more healthily, and by doing that they will heal our planet?"

"Children are the special ones. They are the ones with imagination and can make change. If they eat the right foods, their minds and bodies will evolve to another level. They will have better protection against illnesses and diseases and have the potential to become the best they can be. They will grow into scientists who can create new technologies that will help save your planet.

You need to help them get on the right path. Encourage them to eat all the good things your planet provides – strawberries, bananas, oranges, onions, peppers, potatoes, broccoli, carrots – all of them, the full rainbow of colourful fruits and vegetables. Watch in amazement as they achieve beyond their wildest dreams."

In Mr Thinkalot's head, a light bulb suddenly switches on. "So it's that simple. They eat better, we evolve as a race to become the best we can be - by eating more fruit and vegetables."

A big roar of claps and cheering comes from the party, and some hearty slaps on the back. Mr Thinkalot could just not believe the answers have always been right under our very noses.

The music starts again and everyone moves into the middle of the floor. They all start dancing again and the party gets into full swing with everyone in great spirits; eating drinking, dancing and laughing. Mr Thinkalot really enjoys the party and then Wave announces "you have 30 minutes Mr Thinkalot before you must head back to Earth, so I suggest you say your goodbyes."

"I could stay here forever, I'm going to miss you guys" Mr Thinkalot splutters emotionally.

Wave walks over and shakes Mr Thinkalot's hand, "we are friends now."

“You have all made me feel so welcome, so thank you friend.”

He picks up the microphone and says goodbye to everyone in the room. He thanks them for their hospitality, and for being so welcoming and caring.

Wave inquires, “how are you going to convince everyone at home?”

“I’m not sure at the moment, but I must convince them. I will fight till I drop.” he insists. The room erupts in more cheers and clapping.

Mr Thinkalot drinks a tomato juice as Maggie wheels on over, “COME ON MR THINKALOT, LET’S HAVE ONE MORE DANCE BEFORE YOU LEAVE.”

RPC Mike runs up to him and carry’s him to the dancing area, and the three of them throw some moves as everyone else joins them in one last dance.

Mr Thinkalot puts on his ***SUPER SPACE HELMET***, says his last goodbyes and gets himself into position.

Wave adds, "I really hope you save your planet."

"I hope so too. Maybe one day I can help Eden and your planet, Wave."

CHAPTER 14

As he stands in the middle of the dance floor preparing to leave, Wave shouts, "prepare the roof." The disco ball disappears and the ceiling starts to pull back to reveal the dark sky of Eden, ready for Mr Thinkalot to launch.

Mr Thinkalot presses the POWER button on, "Hello Bert."

He presses BUTTON 1, "activating camera mode; check."

The he again presses BUTTON 2, "activating air supply, check."

He gives everyone one last wave. They all wave back at him and then carry on with the party.

He presses BUTTON 3 and activates his rocket boosters. He flies up and through the big open ceiling so fast, into the sky over Eden, before reaching outer space.

"Bert activate the breaks." Mr Thinkalot comes to a complete stop floating high above Eden. "Thank you. Thank you citizens of Eden."

Bert then announces, "I HAVE BEEN QUITE BUSY WHILST YOU HAVE BEEN GALIVANTING ACROSS THE PLANET. I HAVE MADE SOME UPGRADES TO THE SUPER SPACE HELMET."

"So I can hear," says Mr Thinkalot, trying to recall if Bert had always been this talkative.

With new gadgets, gizmos and technology in the helmet, Bert calculates that their arrival back on Earth will be sooner than anticipated.

Trying to stop his brain from asking lots of questions, Mr Thinaklot tells himself off, "now stop thinking and get back to the mission, let's get back to Earth."

He double blinks his eyes to bring up the map, "locate worm hole." The map shows the location, "I HAVE CORRECTLY LOCATED THE WORM HOLE," says Bert.

Mr Thinkalot raises a ginger eyebrow at the change in Bert's manner. "Most odd," he thinks, a lot.

"Rocket booster go," he shouts as he presses the button.

It is quite clear that Bert has also upgraded the rockets. They are super loud and roaring like an angry lion. Then, all of a sudden, Mr Thinkalot is zooming at the speed of sound towards the worm hole, into it and right out of the other side without spinning out of control. And there he is, back in his own, familiar, solar system.

He double blinks his eyes to bring the map up again, "locate Earth."

"EARTH IS NOW LOCATED, PAST SOME OTHER PLANETS AND JUST A LITTLE TO THE LEFT," Bert announces.

Mr Thinkalot zooms past all the planets he had passed on the way to Eden. There is Pluto, Neptune, Uranus, Saturn and Jupiter.

As he reaches the asteroid belt, Bert informs Mr Thinkalot, "I'LL TAKE IT FROM HERE FOR A WHILE."

Amazed, Mr Thinkalot is zipped in and out of the space rocks with ease and without hitting any of them.

After he blasts past Mars, he spots a satellite as it floats past him and now he can see home - Earth.

He gets really close to the International Space Station and sees the astronauts waving at him enthusiastically.

"What a fantastic welcome home."

And then he is back in the Earth's atmosphere, and Bert shuts off the rocket boosters; without being ordered to.

Mr Thinkalot is wondering if the upgrades to the ***SUPER SPACE HELMET*** have somehow included it being connected to his brain.

Freefalling through the atmosphere, faster and faster, he passes beautiful fluffy white clouds, and feels the sun's warmth on his face. He inhales deeply as once again he sees the beautiful blue oceans.

Then he can see the wondrous green land and his own country coming into view; the United Kingdom.

He twists his body and changes direction and aims straight for it, eager now to get home.

The parachute opens automatically and he realises his SUPER SPACE HELMET can now do everything on its own, "how easy will space travel be in future now!"

Mr Thinkalot's legs are dangling like spaghetti as he takes in the panoramic view below him; the true beauty of life on Earth. The fresh air, the green fields and snow-capped mountains.

A seagull is flying by watching Mr Thinkalot very curiously. It is probably wondering what type of bird he is. Mr Thinkalot chuckles and gives a, "Hello, Mr Seagull."

CHAPTER 15

Descending slowly down from the sky, he can see a lot of commotion on the ground below him. There are tanks, police cars, fire engines, ambulances, news crews and NASA all waiting for his arrival. And masses of people - Mr Thinkalot has never seen so many people.

"Oh my, look at all of them. Are they really all here for me?"

As he gets closer to the ground, he prepares his legs and stretches them out.

"Bert, are we ready to land?"

"WE CERTAINLY ARE BUDDY." Bert replies.

Mr Thinkalot raises a quizzical eyebrow, wondering what Bert has done to himself, as he starts his countdown to land, "10,9,8,7,6,5,4,3,2,1."

His feet safely land softly on the ground.

Bert announces proudly, "WE HAVE TOUCHDOWN."

The parachute folds itself up and slides neatly back inside the SUPER SPACE HELMET. Even Mr Thinkalot thinks he looks super cool. Everyone is watching with their mouths open. No one has seen a man land from space without being inside a rocket or spaceship.

All the emergency vehicles and the army tanks are heading straight for him but Mr Thinkalot just stands there waiting patiently, wondering what is going to happen. *"Will there be hysteria?"*

The crowds of people are shouting, "UFO, UFO, UFO." Mr Thinkalot realises this is the second time he has been called a UFO. It makes him think about his new friends on Eden. It also seems that suddenly he is famous - a celebrity, but actually he is not really interested in that. He has much bigger fish to fry.

All of a sudden, he is surrounded by people and vehicles. He can hear a helicopter circling above him. The men from NASA try to pull him away from the crowds of people as the news crews push each other trying to get a good photograph and be the first with an exclusive news story. Mr Thinkalot knows this is the quickest and easiest way to get his message out to the people of Earth.

He takes a little step back from the microphones being pushed in his face. He clears his throat loudly, "herrm herrm. I am happy to talk to you all but please, one question at a time."

There's a constant flashing of cameras – it seems everyone wants to see this spaceman.

A reporter named Andrew speaks first, "NASA has been tracking your signal since you left Earth. They lost sight of you and thought you may have died but then you suddenly popped up again on their radar out of nowhere. What can you tell us, where have you been?"

"Hello Andrew and thank you for your question. My name is Mr Thinkalot and I have been on the most awesome, fantastic space journey. You would not believe where I have been and what I have seen. But here I am, back home in one piece".

A lady reporter named Samantha asks, "Mr Thinkalot, what are you wearing and how did you get into space?"

"I am a professor of science and I live and work in London. I have always had lots of thoughts, questions and theories about the universe. I designed my SUPER SPACE HELMET so I could leave our planet and go into deepest space to find answers to some of those questions and test some of my theories out."

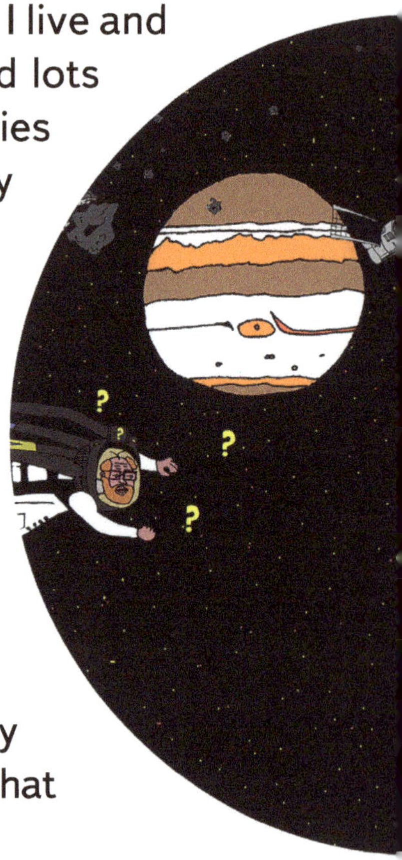

Then a chap called Paul stands up and demands, "and where did you go Mr Thinkalot?"

"I have been all through our solar system. It is so wonderful, absolutely breath takingly beautiful; it's what dreams are made of."

The news reporters are becoming impatient and one called Julie butts in with, "so what happened, where did you go?"

"I have witnessed such amazing things. When I left Earth, my SUPER SPACE HELMET took me on a full rotation around the sun. Then I plotted a trajectory to go far away from here. I passed every single planet in our solar system and located a worm hole.

I plotted a course to go directly into the worm hole. Fantastical as though it may sound, I came out of the other end of it into another solar system. There I discovered another planet. I landed on this planet and found life; it is a planet with a golden city."

Some people in the crowd begin to laugh at him. He has had this for most of his life, but now he is strong and is able to tell his story.

"You may laugh and I am used to that. But I will prove what I say is true." In his head, Mr Thinkalot is thinking that he may have the last laugh.

There's a hush from the crowd as he carries on with his tale.

"This new planet I have discovered is called Eden. The beings there have superb technology, they are far more advanced than we are. They have suffered great tragedies and are fighting every day for survival but have achieved unbelievable things,

I have a message from the leader of the planet, and I need to make you all understand. I have seen the damage and devastation we face if we choose to ignore his message.

Eden was a planet just like ours, full of lush life,

fresh air, seas and beautiful land. They treated their planet as we now treat Earth. They had terrible wars, created pollution with their old-fashioned technology. They over fished the seas and over-farmed the land leaving them barren. They consumed all the planet's natural resources, filling their oceans with plastic and air with pollution. They devasted their world.

They pushed their planet to the brink. It started with earthquakes and tsunamis. Then there was war. Many lives were lost and the land was almost unliveable. The planet's atmosphere began to vanish meaning no plants could grow, the seas became empty of fish, no animals or the inhabitants could breathe.

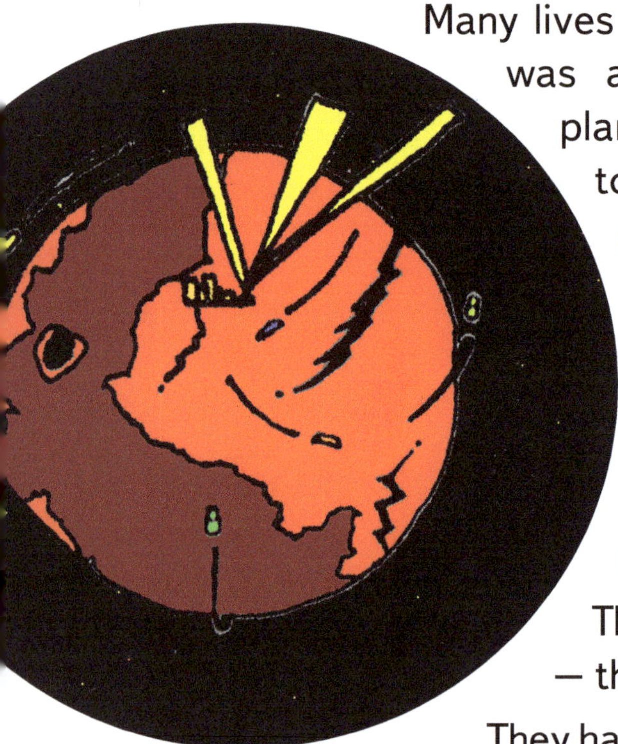

Their world became a barren wasteland.

They just had one city left – the golden city.

They had to think fast, to design a technology for a force field that could be placed over the city capable of holding the air needed for life. They created ways to circulate and recycle air and water for the city.

They developed new, efficient technology to grow all the plants needed to feed their people. They now waste nothing; everything is recycled.

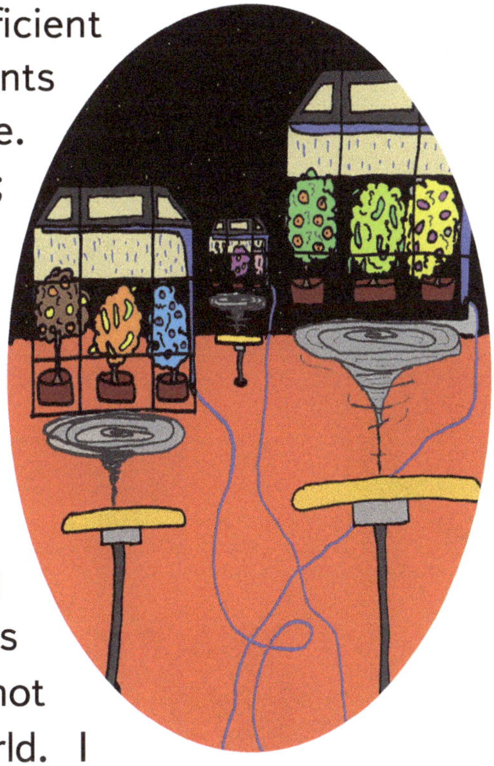

I now see that we are heading in the same direction. Our whole planet needs to work together to create solutions to these problems, find a clean energy, stop taking from the planet, clear the seas of plastics so that we do not destroy this wonderful world. I know we can do this and I have many ideas to help develop the technology we need."

A huge cheer erupts from the crowd.

"We need to stop making things we cannot recycle. We must think ahead rather than just for today. What a waste of humanity that would be as well as the devastation we are causing to other life. Our planet and the life it holds deserves far better than we are doing now."

There are more cheers and then someone shouts out from the crowd, "and how do you propose we do all of this?"

"I know it's hard to believe but it's the truth and I have the answer."

He pauses briefly before carrying on, "the answer is within our children. They are the ones who can save our planet. They are the ones with the creative minds; they are the heroes.

We all need to start eating better but especially our children. Our wonderful planet provides all the good, natural food we need – all the wonderful fruit and vegetables. Why do you think this produce grows at all? It's because the Earth wants us to eat it; mother nature provides everything we need.

Every fruit and vegetable contains all the vitamins, minerals and fibre that have special powers. They help us to fight viruses, bugs and illnesses, they can help cure and protect us from getting ill. We can grow stronger as a species - physically and mentally and evolve to be the best versions of ourselves.

It's only the children who can save us. If they eat better, they will be able to see the problems we face and create innovative solutions to solve those problems. They are our future scientists, engineers and doctors. If they eat rubbish, they will make poor decisions."

A reporter pipes up, "what if we are too late?"

"It is not too late yet. If we start looking after tomorrow today, we might have a chance. I will show some of the evidence in the next few days, so please be patient."

Mr Thinkalot is then led away by security and driven to Buckingham Palace in a huge Rolls Royce car to meet Queen Elizabeth. The Queen wants to see Mr Thinkalot urgently to discuss his **FANTASTIC** space journey and the environment.

The Queen and Mr Thinkalot sit in a large drawing room with a cup of tea talking about his exciting adventures and about what he learned from the citizens of Eden. Queen Elizabeth is very impressed and decides to give him an OBE for his bravery and courage, his work for science and space exploration and especially for the environment.

She holds a huge banquet fit for a king with lots of dignitaries from all over the World. She makes a long speech about Mr Thinkalot's achievements and pins his medal on his white lab coat. He is ever so proud, so much so that he blushes a bright red.

After the banquet, Mr Thinkalot is taken home in a chauffeur driven limousine. He is really glad as he is so tired because he has not slept since Eden.

When he arrives home, he goes into the living room, presses the secret button hidden under the candlestick on his fireplace. The fireplace rotates 360 degrees, opening up into the small corridor. He walks down the corridor to the door at the end. He opens the door and walks into his secret laboratory (remember it's his garage and especially remember not to tell anyone). He takes his SUPER SPACE HELMET off and puts it on the table and says, "well Bert, that was a FANTASTIC space journey. Thank for you for everything you have done."

Bert answers with a yawn, "YOU'RE WELCOME MR THINKALOT. IT'S WHAT I'M HERE FOR."

He throws the blanket over his **AMAZING** invention to cover it and makes his way to bed, banging into walls and tables along the corridor.

Crawling into his bed, he is very quickly asleep.

CHAPTER 16

In the next few days, Mr Thinkalot shows the whole world his evidence that Bert has saved in the ***SUPER SPACE HELMET***. He appears on every TV and radio news programme. People are completely blown away by his achievement. And even Bert has become a bit of a star but he takes it all in his circuits.

On top of being awarded an OBE, Mr Thinkalot is voted as a national treasure of Great Britain and is given a plaque to put in his secret laboratory.

The next few months are very busy for Mr Thinkalot as his life is full of appearances on TV and radio shows but he is always glad to get home though.

The best thing is though, that children and adults all over the world improve their diets.

They eat less burgers, chips and pizzas, replacing them with delicious fruit and vegetable dishes. The government make sure everyone eats a healthier diet by sending free fruit and vegetables to every household.

Children are more creative and involved and all the countries work together to look at ways to create better ways to live without using the Earth's resources. They learn to recycle everything with no waste and the air is becoming cleaner.

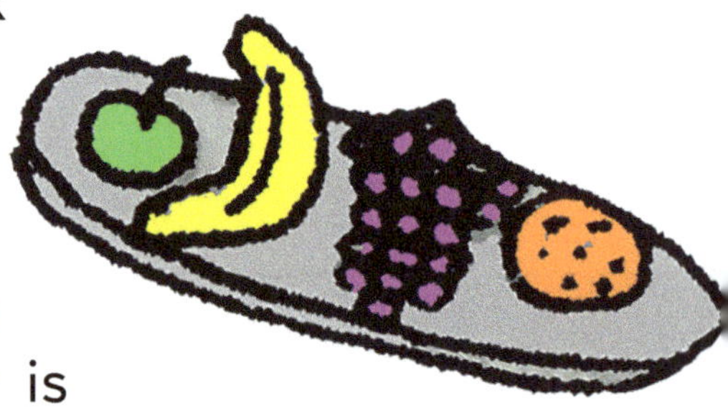

A young girl from the UK designs mini robot drones that search the seas for rubbish and carry it to shore. The oceans are becoming cleaner and the number of fish and sealife is growing. A boy in America creates a new clean energy and over in Japan a girl invents solar powered vehicles.

The children are becoming bigger and stronger, fitter and more intelligent. It is soon clear that they are able to concentrate more and are learning quicker.

They are becoming the best scientists, engineers and doctors - they excel at whatever job they have.

Best of all, children have created the best inventions that are able to solve some of our world's biggest problems.

Mr Thinkalot is very proud.

Everyone has excelled beyond his wildest dreams.

The world is a much happier place.

L
V
RP
RP

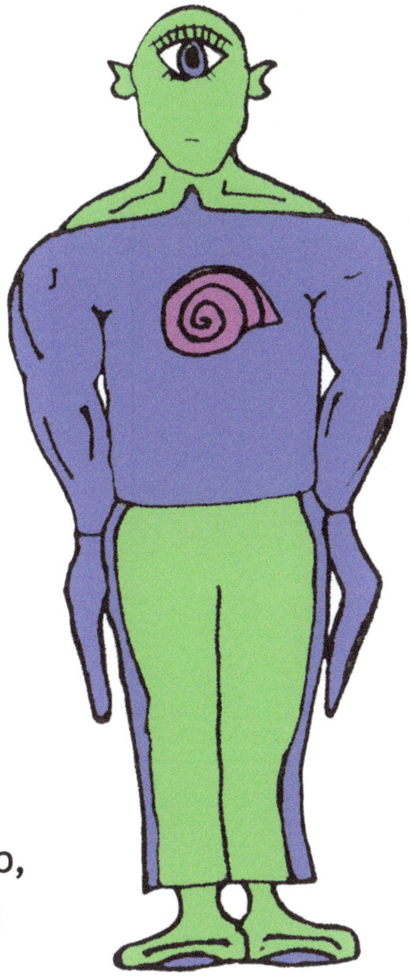

EPILOGUE

One night in his bed fast asleep, Mr Thinkalot dreams of Eden and his friends there; RPC Mike, Maggie and Wave. He yells out in his sleep, worried for their safety.

Meanwhile, downstairs in his secret laboratory, under the cover of his blanket, Bert receives a live message.

"Beep beep, bop. Mr Thinkalot – do you come in? It's Wave, your friend calling from planet Eden."

....To be continued.

DEDICATION

Mr Thinkalot would like to give a big thank you to all the super children out there who are trying all the different varieties of fruits and vegetables. "You are all heroes. Look after our world, innovate, think big, create and enjoy what you do and, most of all, be marvellous."

Lightning Source UK Ltd.
Milton Keynes UK
UKHW050646290822
407872UK00007B/5

9 781912 677986